HEX AND OTHER POEMS

Shane McCrae's most recent books are ⸱⸱ *Sufferea*, a finalist for the Maya Angelou Book Award, the T. S. Eliot Prize, and the Rilke Prize, and *Cain Named the Animal*, both published by Corsair Books. He has received a Lannan Literary Award, a Whiting Writer's Award, an Anisfield-Wolf Book Award, a Pushcart Prize, and fellowships from the Guggenheim Foundation, the National Endowment for the Arts, and the New York Foundation for the Arts. He lives in New York City and teaches at Columbia University.

Hex and Other Poems

Published by Bad Betty Press in 2022
www.badbettypress.com

Cover image: Danse Macabre, Hans Holbein, 1523-5, source: Rijksmuseum

Printed and bound in the United Kingdom

A CIP record of this book is available from the British Library.

ISBN: 978-1-913268-28-2

Supported using public funding by
**ARTS COUNCIL
ENGLAND**

LOTTERY FUNDED

HEX
AND OTHER
POEMS

For Melissa, the miraculous

PRESS

NOTE

The facts regarding the moon's drifting included in "The Moon Is Drifting Away from the Earth at a Rate of Four Centimeters Per Year," as well as the poem's title, were taken from a response written by Corey S. Powell to an inquiry posted on Quora.com.

ACKNOWLEDGEMENTS

Thank you Amy Acre, Timothy Donnelly, Sasha Dugdale, Jonathan Galassi, Alan Gilbert, Derek Gromadski, Jake Wild Hall, Anastasios Karnazes, Dorothea Lasky, Melissa McCrae, Joshua Mehigan, Bradford Morrow, Paul Muldoon, Deborah Paredez, James K. A. Smith, G. C. Waldrep, and Lynn Xu for their friendship and encouragement and support. And thanks to the editors and staffs of the following journals, in which earlier versions of the following poems first appeared:

Cherry Tree: "Inquiry Preliminary to the Examination of Evidence"

Conjunctions: "Hex"

jubilat: "Race in the Body" and "Race in Language"

Scoundrel Time: "The Day the Dead King Spoke the Bomb"

The Yale Review: "Race in the Mind"

My mother is dead. My father is dead
And all the trout I used to know
Leaping from their sad rings are dead.

– W. S. Graham

Contents

Hex

One's opportunities to be unhappy are

Unlimited.   Or limited, but only by

One's own imagination, which is powerful

But fragile, is defenseless,   but is limited

Only by things unseen.   As Bark Psychosis did it

In music, at the start of the new music, *Hex*

Itself the start of the new music, after Talk

Talk started it, who after This Heat started it

Who after Public Image Limited, though John

Lydon has since gone bad, or more offensively

Is who he always was, who after Public Image

Limited started it, going   bad, and not to mention

Slint, not to mention the Americans, Lydon

And Morrissey gone, for   or in Americans

America, for Trump or in Los Angeles

Bad, Morrissey,   not even new, was never new

Except his talent was, and Johnny Marr's,   and always

The dead old art will suffer further life if new

Artists of irresistible ability

Work to extend it,   though such artists must not seek

To extend the   dead old art, or they will fail, but must

Make only what they must   make, and if it aligns

With the dead, the dead will live again in what they make

Low strings,   and keening dissonances when the strings

Ascend together, sirens of the cops inside

Their wooden bodies, their brown bodies. Listen, first

The sirens come from nowhere in the world except

For them, for them the sirens come, announcing nowhere

And then the lights from nowhere round the corner, red

Like an idea of fire, as the drums roll beneath

The strings, a shopping   cart from far from where it rolls

Beneath the city   on a sidewalk in the day

In the middle of the city, roll beneath the city

The strings from which the sirens come, the lights that chase

The sirens down, and live as an idea of fire

And nowhere no guitars.   But space and stillness where

Guitars would be.   Stillness and space and a boy singing

His lone unhappiness in the midst of the raw world

To whom I would escape   from the midst of the raw world

Its now oppressive stillness,   and its windowless

Disease, its timelessness, its timelessness, its nothing's

Happening in my life,   I don't have time to be

Dead, where   to run from timelessness   in the windowless

Room, in the room   in which you sealed yourself   at the start

Of the pandemic, hoping for more life, more time

As Bark Psychosis did it   at the start of the new

Music, and made a sound to which one wanders from

Life,   and in which one wanders still, having arrived

One's opportunities to be unhappy are

Unlimited, though often lately limited

By the end of the world.   But maybe the end of the world is ending

Maybe soon   one will be in small ways sad again

One's opportunities available to one's

Attention, Lydon's to the horseman whinnying

Himself on the fetid, bloating horse, long since afraid

To kick his spurs and pop it,   but he makes an eager

Whinnying, hoping to sound ready. He is ready

To be the last American, whinny and hex

And whinny, hills unfurl beneath him to the hills

Beneath the surface of Lake Erie and the ice

Above the hills   that seems to constitute the lake

From somewhere other than the lake, to be a picture
Of a dead lake, the surface of the thing a picture
Of something else. How far we travel now to be
In the now impossible   presence of things, to which
We ride in light,   that touches and is never touched
All things, by anything, us, even in the light
How far we travel we have traveled to, to watch
The lake unmoving from the parking lot, approaching
The moment, it, the moment   was already in
Our minds accomplished, the long visionary gaze
Across the ice, in the midst of which, the gaze, the ice
Infinite, has no midst, no middle, but is made
Of middles echoing,   in the midst of the gaze, the moment
Through which, the visionary moment, we will leave
Our bodies, gazing, or at least our minds, for once
Won't trouble what we see, such peace accomplished, we
Have known our peace accomplished   on the drive to the lake
And by the time we reach the lake, we've turned around
Already, in our minds, such peace accomplished and
Retreated from, except we park, except we gaze
At the white expanse, and sigh, not knowing which emotion

Demands the sigh, and the sigh leaves us, staggering

A butterfly, our frozen breath, as butterflies

Have staggered, you have watched them, seemed uncertain where

To land, upon which flower, you've watched a butterfly

Choosing,   or if it wasn't choosing, still it seemed

To choose   a flower patterned like itself, our breath

Escaping in the haze of its occasion, you

Watch yours disintegrate and do not recognize

Yourself.   But I am watching and I see you breathing

And watching   I can't see beneath the picture of

Awe on your face, the image of the visionary

Moment, and even if it isn't happening

Beneath the image, I forgive myself for feeling

Nothing, no visionary moment, seeing yours

And the hills roll beneath the surface of the lake

As Mogwai did it, no   singing but in guitars

And sometimes human voices singing, keyboards sometimes

In 1997, three years after *Hex*

At the start of the new music, each guitar a wall

And hammer, both. If   we forgave ourselves for making

What we have made, we would destroy what we have made

Before we'd let ourselves enjoy it, no, we won't

Release ourselves to joy with our forgiveness, never

And so we build a tower from the top of which

We hope to reach forgiveness.   Opportunities

For one to be unhappy are unlimited

A pitch of silence in the everyday unsounding

One's opportunities   belong to one, but rogue

Unhappinesses claim their midsts in a consuming

Infinity that even now approaches yours

As Enya did it, though you didn't notice.   Listen

The songs are hits, but listening, the sure connections

Between all things become long clouds.   America

The sure connections fray in clouds at the Capitol

And those who scream they want you back have never seen you

And wouldn't recognize you if you came,   and those

Who lie face down on the floor in the chamber see the floor

Only. The woman   on the other side of the door

Wide-eyed and bleeding, sees no metaphors. O music

Where have you fled? O music, who will make you new

The Day the Dead King Spoke the Bomb

The day the dead king spoke the bomb

Into the ear of the man who counts the fuses

A Saturday, began like Friday had

The man who flattens the graves chose his

Favorite tractor from a row

Of tractors nobody but him   could tell apart

The one he knew because

It waited always at the farthest right

Of the row, the man who didn't know

For years his sons had repositioned all

The tractors every night, between

Whom, after the man dies, hatred and kill-

ing will obtain   until a judge

Invalidates their claims to his estate

He dragged the flattener across the graves

The shallow grave of the baker caught

(His head) between the spokes of the wheel

Of the carriage of the king, the baker bowing

He flattened carefully as the gilt lawn of the tomb

Of the king, which, every morning

After he flattened it, the man would spray

Paint gold again, as flecks of gold

From the tires of the tractor glittered on

The neighboring graves, in which the dead had rolled

To face away from the tomb, and covered

Their withered ears, the day the king was buried

Who shouted for a phone   into his panic phone

Who shouted *Can you hear me*

Into the Earth itself, face down and rigid as

A soldier at inspection

Arms at his sides, his eyes shut tight, who

Shouted *I won't be killed by an election*

Who shouted till the desk of the man

Who counts the fuses shook   as it had never shaken

Before. He set aside his book

He thought his instruments were broken

He searched the desk,   but he found only fuses

He couldn't say for sure were   not attached to bombs

He pressed his ear to the desk

And heard the shouting from the tomb

And started, sat   upright, afraid

But soon he pressed his ear to the desk again

He thought the shouting was the fuses shouting

    With the voice of the dead king.   The man

    Who counts the fuses listened to

    Their furious noise, then raised his head

Slowly and made a note on the calendar

Beneath the plastic on his desk, *The dead*

    Now speak with the voice of the dead, the fuses

With the voice of the king. Could this technology

Be used to make remote   bombs more effective

    And marked the day with a quick star

Inquiry Preliminary to the Examination of Evidence

Where is it, whiteness, not   whiteness itself

But each of the many   personal whitenesses

Located? *On*   the body? *In*   the body

Or both?   Both but it only   exists between

Two bodies, two or more.   If only two

One white, one any other color. If

More, then one white,   plus any other number

Of any other color   bodies, all

Together in a space. If not,   the bodies

Of any other color must in their

Space know   where always in   what space, what

Position, must   at every moment know

Where the white body is,   and in what atti-

tude. The white body needn't know the at-

titude   of the one or of the more of any other. Measure it. The space   between

What one white body   sees and what will be

True about what it sees is briefer than

The space between the waves that hang a word

On air and the thin air on which it hangs

Measure it. Take   the measure of it hanging

The White People in My Blood

What do I know about the white

People I don't know   in my blood

Does their blood pale my father's where

It meets his blood

Where in my body   does the pale

Blood meet the dark blood?   In my heart

How red   might it have been were my

Blood pure,   my heart

Which red? How much   of which red red

A pale   red, or a dark red,   blood

Red,   heart red? White   blood white as blue day

In the heart,   black blood

In the heart,   black as the breathing sundown

My father's father's father's heart

Might all day long have pounded toward

Then through, whose heart

Kept him awake and running all

Night,   might have, or his father's blood

Rushing, if either ran.   Who runs

Still in my blood

Who chases?   Whose blood darkens where

They meet? Who fights still   in my heart

For what?   What violence is the beat-

ing of my heart

Race in Language

Look back   a generation, I look back

    Ten generations on my mother's side

Further, to England and to Ireland

    Knowing ten words they knew, a thousand words

Knowing the language they, my ancestors

    Knew on my mother's side, in Ireland

In England. I look back   two genera-

    tions on my father's side, his mother and

His father, and I'm sure I know them, most

    Of the words they knew. I can't look back and know

Their fathers or their mothers.   I can guess

    Six generations back,   or seven, too

Many far back past   seven, back   at eight or

    Further, I might not, if I stood before them

Any   who lived in Africa, I might

    Not know a single word.   What could I say

What object could I,   if I stood before

    Them, any ancestor,   what object could

I gesture to, to   start to learn the language

    Wherever I have met them, if I stood

Before them,   any one, if there were trees

    There, I could touch a tree, say   *Tree*, then point

To them, then back to the tree,   or thump my chest

    And say my name, or say *You are my aunt*

Or say *You are my father many fathers*

    Before him.   What are we?   What is your word

For you?   What do you know about the ocean

    If he lived inland.   If he lived beside

The ocean, if   whatever carried me

    Through time to him   could keep us there forever

I could stand listening forever, between

    Him and the ocean.   I could stand forever

Race in the Body

To live and not   to understand
My body, who it lives. To live
Allowed   the black of the blackness of
    The back of my black hand

A gift   of the back of my own hand
Upon which I can balance things
But can't hold them,   and not the pink
    Of the black palm I hold

Now toward you, now toward you
And almost   it's your own outstretched
Hand in a perfect darkness, which
    You now can't place, can't know

In the perfect darkness   in the un-
familiar room.   The feeling you
Can't   place your hand,   that's really you
    Not knowing how the room

Is furnished, will   you stumble over

The heart of the room, a thing   so low, if

You hadn't gone the way you're going

    You would have passed forever

Over it, your hand forever   float-

ing in an atmosphere above

The possibility of touch-

    ing   that which, were you not

A stranger here, could only seem

Strange if you looked at it too long

A low or   in a corner thing

    That makes the room the room

It is, the   bed, the television

Or the long, shrouded desk, upon

Which once, but how could you have known

    A neighbor laid a twitching

Animal, broken, sticky with

Blood, nobody would   say it was blood

Except out loud, nobody inside
    Themselves,   instead they shout-

ed it, their   panic carrying
The blood away, each shout the body
Of the word,   *Blood!*   neighbor and children
    And parent, someone brings

Paper towels and a cup
Of water from the kitchen, later
No one remembers who, tap   water
    Whoever it was stopped

To choose a ruined cup,   from the back
Of the cabinet, the   children clean
Their brushes in it, when they paint
    Stained water   pales the dark

Blood as the shuddering animal
Dies, from which cup   only a stranger
Would drink.   Where is the heart?   With the lights on
    You see no stain at all

Race in the Mind

1.

At five, I thought the best of both

Met somewhere in my body, my

Black father, my white mother, her

Parents had taught me to believe

    Niggers were athletes

2.

When at their best. It wasn't fair

To force white   boys to play against them

But whites were smarter, law-abiding

Not loud, and good,   for whom *good* always

    Meant *better*, boys

3.

And women, who were girls or women

Never white girls or women,   not

The way white boys were *white boys*, women

Or girls,   for whom *good* always meant

    White boys and *silence*

4.

Except for when aggrieved,   or when
Exemplifying, white   women, dying
As I was dying, separately
But separately.   I thought the best
              The strength   of the strongest

5.

And the intelligence of the more
Intelligent,   had merged in me
Somewhere in me, invisible
But certain, certain as my skin
              Was mine,   but certain

6.

Sure as the blackness of my skin
Belonged to someone else, my white
Grandfather, who,   when he was young
Would drive to Eugene, he and his friends
              To jump black students

7.

Young black men walking anywhere

Alone, sure   as the blackness of

My skin belonged to him, and to

His friends, whom I had never met

     Who owned my skin, yet

8.

Had probably never heard of me

Skin meaning the   idea of blackness

I had been taught, *skin*   meaning me

All skin, whatever color,   winds

     Meeting in the whirlwind

9.

Whatever color,   all skin, all

Species, plus human,   for the sake

Of argument, so that one, late

At night might lean in   close to another

     And ask, *Say you're*

10.

Dying,   man, you need surgery
Bad,   in some shithole town in the middle
Of nowhere, do you let a nigger
If he's the only   doctor in

      Town, cut you open

11.

To which the other, where you think
A laugh should go, he doesn't laugh, his
Voice serious, replies, *I'd die*
And take the nigger with me, for

      Argument's sake,   or

12.

They're drunk,   or wish they were, and can't
Say what they'd say if they could say
Anything to each other, my
Grandfather's friends, two, in the night

      In the light from the porchlight

13.

Who owned my blackness like they, one at

least,   owned the porch, the beers, the light

That dies at the edge of the yard,   or it

Continues imperceptibly

        Forever, from the

14.

Porch to the night beyond the sky

Who owned the things they owned as thor-

oughly as anyone can own a

Thing not a human body,   meaning

        their own, the things

15.

They owned   rotting beneath their feet

And rotting in their hands, and rotting

Between the yard and the unbounded

Dark, not the opposite   of the white

        Light, but its limit

The Moon Is Drifting Away from the Earth at a Rate of Four Centimeters Per Year

But 50 billion years from now the moon

Will stop, its orbit will have gotten as

Big as it's going to get, a 47

-Day lunar month, one day, you won't

Feel it, the moon will stop, the moon will

Snap into place, one day, and drift no farther

From us, away, the earth, us, and the moon

Won't anymore affect the tides, the sun

Will move the oceans and the moon will only

Watch, its face lit by the sun, the oceans swaying

Except the sun by then, by 50 billion

Years, just 5 billion years   from now, the sun will

Have swollen and consumed the earth and moon

5 billion more or less, or changed in such

A way the drifting of the moon away

To all the way away won't happen, or

The oceans will be stripped from the face of the earth

Where are you going do you think you're going

It has been theorized the moon was struck

From the earth, was torn from the earth, was struck

Away and that was how the moon was made

All its existence   has been one explosion

And every poem one report, was struck

Away,   even now you see the moon recoils

From violence at the source of which you stand

In the pursuing darkness in a forest

Far from the city,   you have come back home

Elated at first, driving, and the distance

Seemed, as you passed beneath the traffic lights

At what had been the first real intersection

You recognized it, but the waste land where

The waste land used to be, the last quick mile

Before the intersection, green but ragged

But green and ragged, now was shops and one

Gas station where you used to wish a gas

Station would be   when you were seventeen

But seeing it as you approached the first

Real intersection, what had been the first

But now it was the third or fourth, you lost

Your sense of where you were,   but even so

Elated, though the distance seemed, the distance

From the city to your   hometown seemed so short

It passed so quickly you, arriving, wondered

Whether you had ever gotten all

The way away, though everything had changed

The town had changed, and now was unfamiliar

And if you hadn't gotten all the way

Away where have you been, because, if so

You haven't, all those years since college, been

In the city, where,   but where have you ever lived where

You felt your body altogether was

Yours,   separate from the place where you were living

Or not   yours, but a part of the place, if ever

Either, not either   since you were a child

You've always been a moon of where you've lived

And after, right away, after you passed

Through the once first,   now third, fourth intersection

A panic overcame you and you swerved

A panic overcame you and you tried

To turn around, you   jerked the wheel to the left

And swerved, what will the city be when you

Return, if, leaving, you have brushed away

The cataract of its familiar changes

You needed to get back,   and almost swerved

Into a long blue car the color of

A cloudless sky at noon in early spring

Tailfins, four headlights, wide,   older than you

Alien,   and you swerved, and the long car

Swerved, though its driver didn't turn his head

Till hours later, night, when he was sitting

He's sixteen, and he's sitting   at a bright

Window in a bright house   at the edge of the dark

Forest.   The full moon clarifies the bare

Branches through which you see the house, how bright

The window is, how bright it is, how bright

Milton Keynes UK
Ingram Content Group UK Ltd.
UKHW010155050324
438811UK00005B/102